PINK REEF

ROBERT FERNANDEZ

CANARIUM BOOKS
ANN ARBOR, STUTTGART, IOWA CITY

SPONSORED BY
THE UNIVERSITY OF MICHIGAN
CREATIVE WRITING PROGRAM

PINK REEF

Canarium Books
Ann Arbor, Stuttgart, Iowa City
www.canariumbooks.org

The editors gratefully acknowledge the
University of Michigan Creative Writing Program
for editorial assistance and generous support.

Cover: Evan Gruzis, *Color Blind*
2008, India ink and watercolor on paper, 28" x 20"
Used courtesy of the artist.

Design: Gou Dao Niao

First Edition

Printed in the United States of America

ISBN 13: 978-0-9849471-3-3

for Mary

CONTENTS

PINK REEF

*

I chose
pink reef surging toward
the name of the dog

pink reef shedding under the tree,
snapping at masks

. . .

I wanted to understand
this ethos of cameras
strung through juniper leaves,

juniper lenses seeing
at the tops of the trees:

a bread
of violets
baked in

a bread
of mussels
glutting the

a cache of
roe in the
stomach

*

I will reform,
re-encounter love's law
I will follow
after the bright
seeds of marrow are
shaken from the thigh
& the thigh placed
on a stick in
the faceless gallery
I will devote,
for thou hue
thou gravel
thou hearse—
the blood oranges
so bright
because they are
against a white
background
the blood oranges
so bright
because they are
against a white
background
the blood oranges
so bright
because they are
against a white
background
the blood

oranges
cold and light
cold and light
cold and light

*

why do I
choose to turn away

why do I refuse
why am I refusing

we want to steal me away
we want to surgery me

why don't they
steal me away

red refrigerator-blood
fills me

*

child this way
I wake and believe
I am abandoning forever

young marksman, I forget chilled pasta
by Ida Applebroog

I forget the cobras
in a blanket

I forget

the red roe
of *ekstasis*

I forget the unholy
mouths of the iguanas

*

suddenly the colt
bisected by

suddenly the chest of the colt
peeling away

suddenly
the panic

of such a mass
loose in the hands

suddenly this is
mine this is mine this is
mine

our folds, our
welling of red
roe in the eyes

our pecking
gold parrotfish
of the real

*

whose loss is your refusal
whose refusal is your light
whose laughter reveals
the event or
luminous ouroboros appear
every time the crocodiles are around

take a lesson,
realize we are
not all children
of the damned

understand
the damned
in Duino
on vacation

understand
the damned
with sails unfurling
from their
assholes

take a lesson
from what it means to say
what you are not
(what you are)

*

First breaking the black ossetra candies of
Enmity, first the ecstasy's Versace and sand-dry, first
Rustle of closed eyes, first
Noon of soft Versailles,
And Erik Satie on the speakers,
Noon of thunderhead Satie and horns in the sawed-off
Distance, noon a pyramid of dry
Eggs on the back, high noon of heat and dry
Zephyr

*

father,

I am gold,

a great grey
owl with

the soul's
face,

soul's
face

of the great grey owl's
shirred

facial
disc

everything
swivels &

slips
everything

shines

*

I am a piece of the wall
or a big blade crosses my arteries, defleshing them

I am a stabbing
I am a big part of the wall comes fucking me

blood poodles in the fountains
I am happy to have continued
happy to have worked

*

like the father splits
his tongue down the middle

like a dog laps at the blood
like there is an ink

into which seeing passes:
an ink

of vultures
pocked in mist

an ink like
a cuttlefish of the fist

*

trying to get
a maximal grip:
I want to stop

I am the
blistering *qualia*
of all that lives

I am a slot filled with meat,
but that is not money

there are nautiluses
in the corn,

but the nautiluses
spray debris

bull draped in a mirror
of sweat

sprays corn
& blubber

I am listening
to whale song
in the alien corn

*

happily I explore
bunches of

cherries under the
happily I explore

banquets of paradise
roses inside of

happily
from Paris

their son a
little bunch of roses

*

I am shrill,
barking through

a waterfall
at black rock

these odalisques
on the moss

take their color
from the falling water
& the sky

take their color
from the snakes
that cool themselves

& drink
between the rocks

take their color
from the fine
mist,

the rainbow's
light

*

one is not to cower

one is to stand straight

one is not to cower

not to ease or

release

one is to grip straight

one is to tense right

one is to grit

the straight teeth

one is to tense

& arc the blood

one is to style

& tense the blood

one is to grip right

*

to hell with those that
hand themselves over

the vents are warm
to hell with those that

hand themselves over
to me to hell with those that

hand themselves over

to hell with those that
hand themselves over

to me
that warm themselves

in me

*

eat glass,
swallow blood

heart swallows glass,
blurts blood

bubbling is endless

heart surrounded
by red bubbles

heart surrounded
in delicate lights

heart flexing
on a trident

*

& am seeking
the bleeding vent

get me on my feet,
help me stand

the roads are black,
the roads are iced,

the roads are choked
with snow

the roads are
staggered meat,

fresh ribcage
of a deer

what is meat
to common

"shall suffer"?

what is meat to
sides of venison

covered in moths?

*

just the soldiers
just the eels flayed &
diced
just the artist at
thirty-one
just the blood baked
into cookies
just this *louche*
that gluts on
blood and drops
from the ceiling
just the Colombian
roses wrapped
in butcher paper, stuffed
into refrigerated
planes
just the splayed stent
that is your
laughter
just the tube
through which
the worm flows
just
the world
is coming
to an end
just the gut smiling
from its bloated,
blood-cheeked

grin
just the smiles
(just the smiles)
just the smiles

*

gestalt psy-
chologists
thinking
the brain's
grooves
correspond
to
(instress
bursts
from you
like a fish)

& what
a treasure of blood,
what human
blood in that ray

what an emperor
of the dolphin's
black blood
stamped
into coins

what beings
embodied
in our style
(when a sting
ray advances
the wrists

spread their
lips)

what does it then mean
to say
the organs
look prettier on the outside
or that a sick Medusa
huddles herself
in a corner of the new
Fontainebleau?

*

it is
epic (humpback
washes ashore
with signs of decay)
it is
a Coriolanus
it is
a coronet it
is a trumpet
a diadem
it is Night's
Queen in her
raiment of stars
it is aphasic,
minor (picking
leeches
from the throat)
& the blood
will remain
as ever
the blood will remain
as ever
& the blood
will remain
as ever
souls

*

if trying too hard is to be
unfeeling and thankless
if it is hard where then

do you hide your kernels
where then devil do you
release your sheets

where then ornament,
where can I trust my eyes

where then lying
are you light, are you down,
are you dolmen, liquid
crown

where then
your power to charm
me your power to see me

I awake in affair I again
in a day I remote and de-
mote I flurry and fathom

I gust up in fathoms
as in a net
I bring you fathoms

*

trading disaster for the hope
of panicked black silk fleeing down the mountain

I can muster my kind of silk (lavenders
no longer smell as sweet)

I can get the veins to work (pumping
purple silver smells as sweetly)

I can organize the purple Versailles of my
disaster (purple halls of mirrors

might smell as sweet)

*

nude peeling away strips of suntan
tracking shot
nude peeling away yellow clouds, caftans
nude peeling away black plaid rubber boots
tracking shot
nude peeling away the curtains of Solomon

I have compared thee, O my love,
to a company of horses in Pharaoh's chariots

I have compared thee, O my love,
to a smear of gold teeth in Pharaoh's chariots

I have compared thee, O my love,
to a gold eye dreaming in Pharaoh's chariots

& it is that we are alive
it is that we are fallow
it is that ecstasy's
gas masks flop
from beneath our ribs

*

imagines itself
a Cadillac-
mouthed cupid,
imagines
it entices with its
rosy skin (this morning
as ever
the wine
is black,
this morning
warlocks
walk through the walls)
this morning
as ever (O
Wolfgang)
we are
stilled before
a wall of speakers

you would imagine
yourself
not devious
deranged,
corrupt or
corrupting,
rather joyful,
fair

you would imagine

yourself
waiting for
the unknown,
for what
cannot
be expected

*

all's ghost
& Lord
noise &
abyssal jet
O Lord
I am
my brothers,
red ibis sunning
its wings
& sea-grapes
heaped on the dock,
a rib of heat rising along
the opaque surface
of the water

*

traveling
in saffron clay,
the colt,
tendons
torn, wants
to rest but is
driven relentlessly
on
(our knight
rides his horse
to death, steals
another, rides on)
it is as if the colt, peeled
from tawny film, is mist
gnashing across clay
it is as if the colt
mends, becomes
lighter

*

I've decided to pay
just at the point
I've decided
to pay into
the linen wall
& hope the fountain
will take my money

just at the point
at which I've decided to pay,
the point at which
the slit begins to leak
(it must be
a gusher)

just at the point
at which
the pigeons circle
around the single
violet pigeon
as if slowly
tending a star

just at the
point I want to stop:
the wall is amber

just at the point
I see the vultures

in the distance
& am given back

just as liars
bleed from
the eyes

just as
at any moment
I like to play
at being desperate

as at any moment
being desperate
likes to play
at being
brained

so the brain corals
heave
through the arms,
budding
across the skin
(torso by
Cimabue)

just so I ask
for the peace
to be &
simply is

& ask for
the peace to be
among my stung
with buds
brother
cacti

*

was the black wallet
was the moral
was the quilled
meat of the wallet
was the vernal
floes of light
was the murder at
the site of production
red heart steaming
bleeding in the hands
red heart of
silk organza streaming
bleating thread
red heart of
polished metal
streaming, unspooling wet
sheets of metal . . .
Jeff Koons
places a hand
on my lung
I say
I know
I am not
adequate
my stomach
would bleed
into a gallop
Jeff Koons
wants to fuck me

I offer him
a strip of
my back,
a strip
of my bloodied
bleeding

*

sensitive anti-discourse dolphin
with your graceful pink

penis sensitive
expressivist teller of tales

with your pregnant precarious
dolphins

master of manners radical
chic with your rabid

drifting *joui-*
ssant dolphins

sensitive visionary master
of manners sensitive

softly so real so
funny really I

get so sick of myself I
want to clip &

clop, clip-i-
ty clop

*

never again second-guessing my
"I am loves"

& the horses walk off,
sweat hardening

what is it to ruminate,
to boil over? The blood

like a net,
we dredge up

(Catullus) radishes
& mullets

*

why don't I hope that I hate my-
self, says Judith, cutting a Madonna
nook out around her sternum

why don't I blast blood
from between my teeth, says
Judith, rubbing her naked feet together

why don't I just die, says Judith,
drawing a dozen roses *ta-
da* from beneath her ribs

*

red blood that runs
through the mahi's veins

the blood an aureus
on which Agrippina's nose is up-
curled

your
body on the cleaning board
cut then grip the gills'
shag,
tear loose

there is meat enough for us all for all of us lush
medallions

*

it is the refulgent blush of your experience
that tends fires with Visigoths and swans

it is the blush that makes you ornery
(you make me
work harder for my lilies,
you make me reflect on my scent of meat)

it is the refulgent blush of your
diadems that makes me itch through the scrim-
shawed ant-hill of my bones

it is your blush that makes me
ornery, that blushes with the cheetah foam
of my refulgent disasters

*

the artist
has blood in the stomach

the artist has
blood &

bubbles of blood
in the stomach

the artist has
organs announcing themselves
as organs

I cannot argue with the flesh
I cannot argue with the meat
across which I speak
across which I grapple
& beat

*

draw the jaw back
shake the eyes
back into the head
tear back the meat
joining the jaw
to the cheek
an egg emerges
in the cheek
observe the egg
in the pocket

*

bent over,
spitting
avocado seeds

we should be happy
releasing seeds,
glass screens
lifting from the seeds
(the pearl and wrapped
Pegasus of the face un-
wraps its wings)

releasing seeds
to not be sick

we should be happy,
voiding them

*

a pot of soil
mixed with

charcoal and egg-
shell:

in the first instance,
the orchid is a mask

*

leave the weed
untended,
it becomes a tree,
becomes a trunk
(a gray &
black flower
blossoms
from its crown)

leave the weed
untended,
it reveals
a face (O
man walking
beneath the leaves
O eyes shaded
beneath a broad-
brimmed hat
O lean
silhouette)

then a shock of rain,
an ecstasy of sudden passage

*

eyes burn from the acidity
farther off

cock splits into plump
lilies

jasper is mixed with the milk,
raccoon is mixed with the water

harbinger of little
blood discs

I am going
coming
seeing
laughing

I run my hand
over the red backs
of dolphins,

over baked
lilies

the lilies are tan
& plump this afternoon

*

spins
an ethics
of banana-leaf
packets in which
moist cakes
cook

spins
the linga
& tulip together

spins
trans-
national
pools of
soft orange suns
flexing over pebbles

or spins the searchlights
that drift screaming (all my
Marilyns are trapped in the light,
all my Marilyns . . .)

*

soup is
all the good stuff
mixed in,
soon enough,
the froth,
tomato-
white, mixed
with cubes
of eggplant,
some
"nail your
hand
to the
refrigerator"
brittle,
some "one
who betrays . . ."
I must power down
these lights,
flush the light-discs
from my chest

*

in the streets,
the macaws, actually, they are
everything working against us
& have been for months

what, besides, shall we make
of slews

slews of
crowd crystals

I get tired
I get exasperatingly lost
I think, here I had it in my hands
now, all my souls broken into
qualities

I need
a rest;
the vultures
along the wall:
tethered with gold thread

I am leaving the world
I am entering the
sotto valley

*

always skylight cubes, melting
Les Demoiselles d'Avignon cubes

Les Demoiselles d'Avignon
blocks of melting shine,

gushing arcades
of blond and red reef . . .

water flows over me,
light flows out of me

*

so soon
into chattering and lounge
quite soon
too soon
rye light
rye eye seeing as it's flowing
flown ground eating
across seeing
find the dragon's scales seeing in
my stomach's bleeding

*

believe everyone you meet, wipe
the blood up from the street
eat acid in the heat, expel
warm white tracers

split the grain of the light,
we
get fucked up every night

watch the Glory mites
eating away at our
seeing

*

angels of "how exactly am I feeling?"
ask yourself
ask yourself
"how exactly am I feeling?"
I cannot stop I love hell
I am light
new moon again but I am light
Cartier chariots strung with pearls
expelling billowy brown light
I cannot stop
fucking
loving

*

Mais où sont
les neiges d'antan?
Villon in
a flame mask
ratchet the cheeks
into matricide
Villon face
down in the snow
knows what sweats blood is like
to be damned

*

in dry leaves,
leaves
wormed as of
cinder spreading
across gums, traveling
mouth of rimmed flame,
mouth of fragrant smoke,
mouth of bonded leaves,
of eggs and seeds,
of rustling
& papery meat

*

eel coiled around
the throat

crimps my
stomach

loosens
my voice

does not
account

for laughter
or the scream

the scream boils like
regulator bubbles
under ice-pack,

collects in
faults

the seals
swallow them,

drink them

like coffins

*

I grit the gift,
get at the soul
I am curious

really we love
& wander
toward forgetting

really we
tinted windows
& why not?

on the beach
at sunrise
unraveling
bulb across bulb
of radiance

unraveling
folds of
so soul
I blister

so so
I see

red tents of
unbearable light

*

if the boy
emperor
comes forward with his
glass crown,
if the boy pharaoh
comes with his
white-peacock winged
chariot

if in
the failure
& a season of rest,
if in the failure
& the season
we are
damp holes
through which
the length of an arm
may glide

homelessness
is our becoming
first a camel
then a lion
then

homelessness
rolling us
between the sun

& sapphire vault,
between (eter-
nity)
sun mixed
with sea

*

in light-
showers,

a pod of seals—
thick

as thick-souled meat—
crowds the rocks

& there is no need
to convince you

of the pleasure
thinking

into you,
there is no need to warn

you: your silver
bricks unravel

*

we become soft
light in purple wafers,

a depth of
indigo-Caribbean,

blue holes

in the limestone
plateau,

& spirits,

black-clear,
blue-grey,

welling
from limestone punctures,

loas,
manta rays,

pooling
in limestone fountains

*

daimon,
really I'm gusting
toward

really I'm
plenary
I'm affirmation

really I
O daimon of abandon

daimon of fluency
& of love

O plenary abandon

*

we hoist the dolphin
onto the dock
run our fingers
across it, we
quarter it
the meat is deep
red at the edges
the meat
is bright pink
between the spine
& ribs
the meat
is dusty
moth wing at
the edges,
curling
bare jaw
& broad skull
the meat is
coffee colored,
misty-
white
we quarter
the back
& belly
of the dolphin
we gather
the blood
in buckets
in shiny strips

*

happiness,
you see I am
trying to get
my back straight
I am trying to
shear off
my spine's
hangnails
happiness,
you see I am
trying to
uncoil
the
rings
around
my tailbone
happiness,
I
have
marrow
like Christmas lights,
marrow
like rubies
& salts heaped
on a square of cloth

*

while I was in my cradle
a vulture came down to me,
& opened my mouth with its tail,
& struck me many times
with its tail against my lips . . .

& if the wood breaks
into violets, none of us
sure enough to speak but of
those violets there was a name
sometimes thoughtlessness,
a gust of air, or flame
drawing its nets into starlight

& if the wood is flame,
it brittles when it sees us,
it breaks into fire-ants and violets

& thus I ask you,
should we not
work? I ask you,

if we have bread
then why not bake
the bread into violets?

*

in names I pass, in pleasures,
shoulders seen from the beginning

we remain rain, remain incomplete,
who of swans in the mind

who can forgive us—black beaks budding—
(who can tell us our names again) how strange to be called:

masses of yellow weather just beyond those hills
egrets beneath lemon leaves just beyond those hills

no one defends us we are our eyes
(how strange to be called F-e-r-n-a-n-d-e-z)

Marietta, combs and sweet cakes just beyond those hills
zinnia and wild rose, acres of flowering just beyond those hills

& in the valleys
        when I wake,
in the valleys when I wake . . .

*

"a bracelet of black

roe about the bone . . ."

not seeds for selling

(a bracelet of fire-

violets) but what

souls sell simply—

least of our burdens,

a crown of

thornapple husks

pressed into her darkest hair

*

the table set, blood
ruptures cloth speakers

the oxtail broth set-
tles (sunrise
ice), no

color-
less ice or
cloth dot that

crushes
sundown's multi-
beaked array—

dusty black
macaw for dinner

black foam from cloth speakers,
black foam, bright sand from
cloth speakers

*

black beads
of sweat rain down, beads
stop the drilling (droplets of

unyielding ore) black droplets of
sweat rain down on houses, on the fur
of sweat-drenched Dobermans

glossy black drops water
the eyes, the teeth fold dull lead, a spray
of black droplets from the mouth is ink &

leathered lion

*

to die is then
glass in the milk and woven through the cheeks—
to die is drier and the milk hotter

what of our feet, & shall they sew
what of our eyes, & shall they sew
what of our cheeks, & shall they sew

who shall dislodge us, braid
that holds the stomach intact
amber droplets that hold the wood-
grain tight

*

Chanel, don't make me laugh I'm trying to die, I'm
trying to drive
while the window's caked in ice and the pink
birthday cake of our deaths sputters Doñas, Doñas
of spine-spread sun, of roe-packed spine,
of bleeding Neros running through
crowds of Doñas—Doñas our bleeding
shall be heard but first we break the back,
first pack the ribs with
eggs

*

certain styles
which are discs, which are
crisp or supple wafers
on which are printed
stars

on which are printed
stars pimpled or rimmed
in tender teeth, in which are
hours drawn crisp or
supple, in which are names
stretched and smoked,
in which are piles
of dried fish . . .

the mounds of roe are
so bright today it's like
I see the sun for the first
time it's like I see the sun clearly
in the idea of it it's like I see the sun
clearly in the black mounds of
shine in the swollen
clear of it

*

how art thou art and tensile
strength and thou art right to style
strength how thou art undone and are not
strength but bitter fungal discs
risen along the waist

sifted or
plainly armored, crocodiles
rise along the bank, golden night falls

on crocodile backs but falls
lightly, falls, settles, and is ingested
but how is style brightly bitter,
bitter torso and bitter bark, styled
skin across which bitter
white discs begin
to lift

*

take
a blade to the brain
coral &

press,
take a hard-
ened stomach (wrinkled

cashew) &
press—

the cameras unpack
Tragiks,

holes so styled
the eyes lice light—

give us a
sense of your
Absolute Last

*

whatever I take
I take into my chest

the invisible worm,
that flies in the night

carries its cut
mouth across Bay
St. and Blue Hill Rd.

leaves its mound
of powdered glass
against the corner store

friends say
the invisible worm,
that flies in the night

burns beneath the scales
of the gumbo-limbo tree

*

first the channel's fine-meshed currents
drawn beneath steel wire and passing cars, first
the pelicans perched on channel markers, and first
the sound of a wet towel falling and hands complicit
in love of the serpent, first golden legs
braided in the grass or is it morning and do we
wake to find, is it morning and do we find
Lament for
the Makers
for form is all,
salt is all, sand, light, and air is all,
Medusa with her brain-coral gaze
at the bottom of the sea is all, sun's
descent is all
& laughing, loosely
laughing, these
bricks
that I collect that stand my spine straight and like a candle
gnashes in laughing, weeps
blisters in laughing—
still none of us
are known

*

some lime-colored

kites narrow and attempt

to track you but there are rows

of razors along your palms and you are

friable as the mint leaves in which you

cool your eyes, you are on the sill broken

with the limes struck by lightning in whose

ballooned and dry chambers wasps have laid their eggs

*

the red clay comes hard: at our backs are the

thinking targets: at our sides are the thinking

stars: at our middles, fibrous sop

& drain of hearts that resist

that release certain tubers certain

hands: what we are speaking of is will

which flowers forward from the throat

which forks which fibrous locks, Januaries

of seeing

*

one who flatters a wound
as if clasping blood
is flat as the wound
in leaf-bricked blood

one who flatters a lyre
clips the spine's fused discs,
spreads the mind's bloodied butter
on flat, brittle, cold dry toast

*

knowing is to see
& to remain tragic
at the heart
of where we are to go

knowing is to plate
the stomach in teak
& to remain tragic in the
heart of where we are to go

where we are to go is strung
with gold wreaths unfolding
as sight at the heart
of where we are to go

knowing is seeing
as art, is travel
in the Attic light
of where we are to go

*

the throat faults
the leather

the stitch sutures the eye
the eye sutures the fault

the eye sutures the cut
in the stomach

the stomach sutured with lashes
the throat pleasures the fault

*

I cannot
I refuse
I refrain
I stay
desert-like
I stay
pimpled mask
I stay
bleached violet
I cannot
I refuse
I refrain
I stay
psalters
of crisp meat
I stay
boggling
swooning
lighting
I stay littoral
dusting
hewn
I
cannot
I refuse
I refrain

AUTHOR'S NOTE

Special thanks to Joshua Edwards, Robyn Schiff, Nick Twemlow, and Lynn Xu. As ever, my thanks to Mary and my family.

Grateful acknowledgment is made to the editors of the following journals in which some of these poems first appeared: *Boston Review*, *The Claudius App*, *Conjunctions*, *Hambone*, *Mandorla*, and *The Seattle Review*.

In certain places poems in this book quote from, adapt, or are otherwise indebted to Thomas Lovell Beddoes, William Blake, Elias Canetti, John Donne, William Dunbar, John Keats, Federico García Lorca, Friedrich Nietzsche, Frank O'Hara, Arthur Rimbaud, Nelly Sachs, Song of Songs, Wallace Stevens, Wolfgang Tillmans, François Villon, and Leonardo da Vinci.

Robert Fernandez is the author of *We Are Pharaoh* (Canarium Books, 2011). He lives in Iowa City.